The
First Peoples

of the Americas

Monica Sevilla

Contents

The Origin of the Native Americans

All of the **Native American tribes** in North America, Central America, and South America are descendants of Asiatic people who migrated from Northern Asia, into Siberia, and across the **Bering Strait** during the Ice Age. during the ice age, the level of water in the seas were much lower than they are today. Much of the Earth's water at

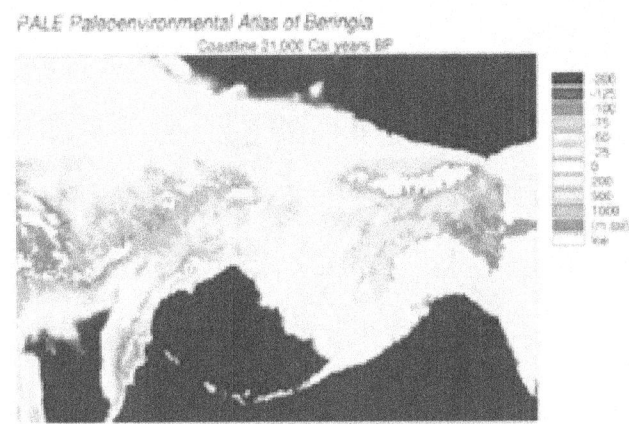

this time was frozen as ice. This caused the land between Siberia and Alaska to be dry and exposed. This occurred from 20,000 to 8,000 years ago. This was a land bridge that was about 1000 miles wide was known as **Beringia**. These ancient people trekked through the tundra to reach Alaska.

The people crossing Beringia were part of a small founding group that gave rise to all of the Native American tribes in the North American continent. Scientists believe that only a few thousand people survived the last **glacial**

maximum in Beringia. The last glacial maximum is the point in history when the ice sheets were at their maximum extension across the North American continent, Europe, and Asia. The last glacial maximum lasted from 26,500 to 20,000 years ago.

They spent 5000 years within this region until the **ice sheets** locking their southward passage melted. Beringia, in contrast with North America, had very low levels of ice. It was a refuge for the people who were living in Siberia. They then migrated south along the Pacific Coast of Alaska around 15,500 B.C.

Knowledge and Comprehension
Words to Know:

The Native American Tribes:

Bering Strait:

Beringia:

Glacial Maximum:

Ice Sheet:

1. Who were the ancestors of today's Native Americans?

2. What is the late glacial maximum?

Application, Analysis, Evaluation and Synthesis

3. Describe how the ancient people of Siberia came to the North American Continent.

4. Explain why did the ancient people of Siberia occupied Beringia for 5,000 years.

5. Why, in your opinion, did the ancient people of Siberia want to migrate into North America? Justify your answer.

Native Americans
with Eurasian Origins

A recent genetic study of a 24,000 year old Siberian boy changes what we once thought about native American ancestry. The prevailing theory about native Americans was that they were primarily east Asian, and that members of this Siberian population group migrated into the North American continent via the Bering land bridge. This new genetic study demonstrates that the genome of this Siberian boy is related to both

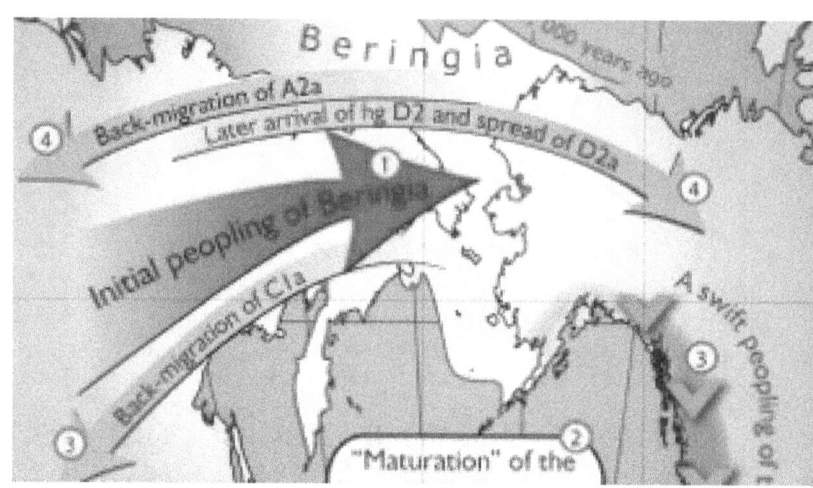

present-day western Eurasian populations and modern Native Americans in the New World.

The skeletal remains of this boy, the oldest genome ever sequenced, consisted of an arm bone. It was found at the

Mal'ta site, located on the shores of Lake Baikal, in south central Siberia. The genome of a second individual, dated back to 17,000 years ago has a similar genome. The DNA reveals genes that are found, at the present time, in western Eurasians in the Middle East and Europe. Approximately 1/3 of the genome has this DNA. 2/3 of the genome has eastern Asian DNA.

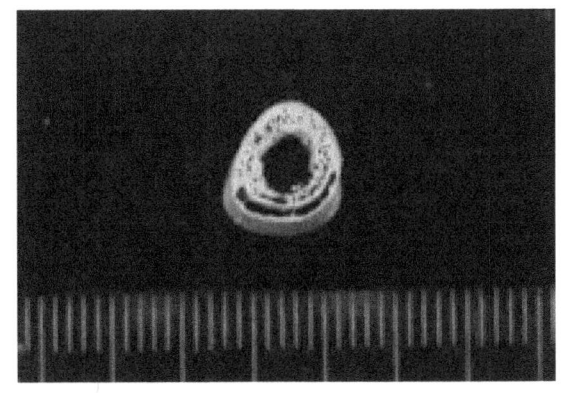

These findings are important because it shows that the ancestors of today's native Americans were a product of two distinct populations: one from western Eurasia and the other from eastern Asia. The genetic mixing of these two ancestral groups may have met in Siberia then migrated over the Bering Strait land bridge, into North America or they may have met in the New World. More analysis of Native American DNA will need to be done to find out where the genetic mixing of these two populations occurred.

Sources:

http://news.nationalgeographic.com/news/2013/11/131120-science-native-american-people-migration-siberia-genetics/

Focus Questions:

1. What is the theory of how the first people from Siberia occurred?

2. Describe what the DNA results of the 24,000 year old Siberian boy were? Why is this important?

3. How do these DNA results change our view about the ancestry of the ancestors of today's native Americans?

4. Where could the meeting and genetic mixing of the two ancestral populations that make up the DNA of the Siberian boy have occurred? Explain your reasoning.

5. What would be needed to have a better understanding of where this genetic mixing occurred?

The Solutreans
America's First Indigenous Americans

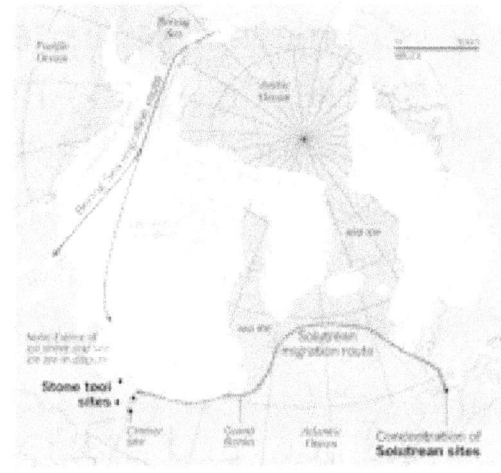

Archeologists have long claimed that the people of Siberia, who crossed the Bering Strait 15,000 years ago, were the first indigenous people of North America. Stanford, an anthropologist from the Smithsonian Institute and Bradley, archeologist from Exeter University have a **hypothesis**, an educated guess, based on their observations and evidence, that suggests that the first Americans crossed the ice sheets from Europe into North America almost 25,000 years ago.

A 22,000 year old mastadon **fossil**, a bone that have been preserved in the rock layers, found along with a human-made **artifact**, a human-made tool pottery, or other product. The artifact is described as a "dark, tapered stone blade close to 8 inches long." The fossil, along with the blade, were both found on Gwynn's island at the southern end of Chesapeake Bay, in Virginia.   The blade matches those made by the ancient Solutrean who lived on the border of in Eastern France and Northern Spain. Five other sites, on the Eastern coast, contained other Solutrean artifacts and stone tools. This evidence suggests that the people who made this blade may have traveled to North America thousands of years before the Siberians crossed the Bering

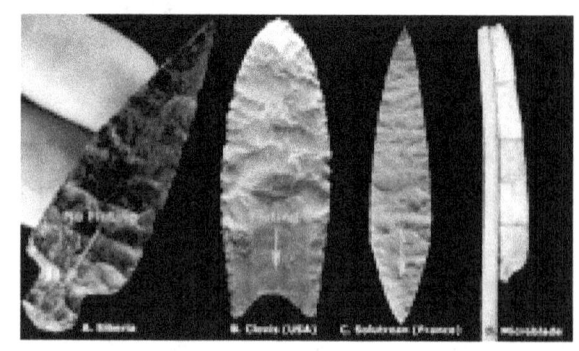

Strait, and made their western migration into the New World.

Stanford and Bradley also suggest that the Solutreans and their descendants eventually spread across the continent to the southeast and east towards New Mexico giving rise to the **Clovis culture**. The Clovis culture also had tools, biface pressure-flaked blades and spearpoints, that were similar in technology to the tools that the Solutreans manufactured. They also state that these tools are not related to the tools manufactured by the indigenous populations descended from the Siberians.

DNA evidence suggests that the Solutreans had a unique mitochondrial DNA **haplotype**, a specific genetic mutation, that the descendants of the Siberian people crossing the Bering Strait did not possess. This genetic haplotype is

known as the X2a marker. This haplogroup mutated from haplotype X2. Haplogroup X2 is known to have existed within the region of the Mediterranean, the Caucasus Mountain range on the continent of Europe, the Orkney Islands in Scotland, and the Israeli Druze community. It is not associated with people from Asia. Stanford and Bradley suggest that the Solutreans may have developed the haplotype X2a marker while in North America. The highest concentration of this

haplogroup in North America is found in Northeastern Canada and Northeastern United States. South Americans do not carry this genetic marker. What this evidence suggests is that the Solutreans migrated into the eastern regions of North America from Europe, via a land or ice bridge in the past and developed the haplotype X2a mutation in North America.

Source:
http://www.washingtonpost.com/national/health-science/radical-theory-of-first-americans-places-stone-age-europeans-in-delmarva-20000-years-ago/2012/02/28/gIQA4mriiR_story.html

Knowledge and Comprehension

Hypothesis:

Fossils:

Artifact:

The Solutreans:

Clovis Culture:

Haplotype:

1. Describe who the Solutreans were and where they lived.

2. What hypothesis do Stanford and Bradley propose?

Application, Analysis, Evaluation and Synthesis

3. What evidence is used to support Stanford and Bradley's proposal?

4. How does this new hypothesis change what we already know about the settling of North America by people who once lived in Siberia? Why is this important?

5. What DNA evidence supports Stanford and Bradley's hypothesis? How is this evidence different than fossils and artifacts?

6. Explain why it is beneficial to have both DNA and material evidence such as fossils and artifacts.

50,000 year old Archeological Site in South Carolina

Ib 2004, University of South Carolina archaeologist Dr. Albert C. Goodyear made a remarkable discovery. Artifacts were unearthed from an ancient pre-Clovis site along the banks of the Savannah River in Allendale, in South Carolina County. The Archeological site, known as Topper, contained pre-Clovis artifacts dated to 16,000-20,000 years ago. One of the artifacts that was found was a chopper made of stone with a bi-facial edge. Digging 4 meters deeper into the sedimentary layer, below an ice age river bed, burned organic matter or charcoal was uncovered in the sediment along with more artifacts. The tools were very basic in nature, unlike the tools found in the upper layers of the site. The charcoal was isolated, taken to a lab, and dated to at least 50,000 years old. The results suggests North America, especially South Carolina, has been inhabited before

TODAY

CLOVIS PEOPLE: 13,000 yrs

RED SOIL: 17 - 19,000 yrs

ICE AGE RIVERBED

PLEISTOCENE TERRACE

2002 Excavation

The Hunters Gatherers of North America

Early humans survived and adapted to many changes in the environment. They became experts at hunting wild game, fishing, and gathering plants and herbs that grew in the wild. They were able to cope with climatic changes, follow wild game, or search for resources such as water, plants for food, stones for making weapons, and other resources. It was an everyday struggle to provide for their basic needs. These **basic needs** included shelter, food,

clothing, and an energy source for cooking food and keeping themselves warm.

These early groups were nomadic or moved from place to place. They followed the wild game such as bison and antelope that they hunted. This was their major source of protein. They would preserve the meat they received from these hunts by drying out which allowed them to eat it for months. They would also use the hides for making clothing, blankets, and use it to insulate their shelters with.

Groups of early hominids as well as members of the modern humans initially lived in caves and rock shelters. Caves and rock shelters protected them from harsh weather such as rain, cold, and heat. It also protected them from wild animals. Later, as they became increasingly more nomadic, following the wild animals they hunted and ate, they began to construct and use temporary structures such as teepees and wigwams that they could take down and move easily from one location to another.

Hominids and modern humans have continuously been using **natural resources** they have found within the environment to meet their basic needs. They were learned where to find these resources and invented different ways to use them to meet their daily needs. They used stone such as obsidian and chert to make tools for hunting animals,

cutting branches and fiber, preparing meat and plants, and chopping plants. Animals have been used for a few different purposes such as for food, making clothing and shelters. The meat is eaten as a protein source, while the hides can be used for clothing, blankets and as a building material. Some of the tools that have been created from bones

such as wrenches, harpoons, needles, awls and batons.

Sources:

http://en.wikipedia.org/wiki/Hunter-gatherer

Focus Questions:

Describe who the hunter gatherer was.

Explain what type of shelters the hunter gatherers lived in when they were hunting and following wild game. Explain why they used this type of shelter.

Identify which natural resources were important to the hunter gatherer.

Describe how the lifestyle of a hunter gatherer is different than your lifestyle today.

What survival skills could we learn from the hunter gatherers to help us survive in the wild? Under what circumstances would this be useful?

the last ice age. This makes the people who lived at this site, the first peoples of the New World.

The long held theory is that North America has been inhabited since 13,000 years ago as a result of a migration from Siberia, across the Bering Strait, and into the North American continent. What this evidence suggests is that the people who lived at this site pre-dated and migrated into North America more than 50,000 years ago.

Source:

http://www.sciencedaily.com/releases/2004/11/041118104010.htm

Smallwood, Ashley M. "Clovis Biface Technology at the Topper Site, South Carolina: Evidence for Variation and Technological Flexibility". *Journal of Archaeological Science* 37 (2010): 2413-2425: 2414.

Snow, Dean R. (2010). *Archaeology of Native North America*. Boston: Prentice Hall. p. 44. ISBN 978-0-13-615686-4.

Focus Questions

1. Describe where the Topper site is.

2. What was found at the Topper site?

3. What do you notice about the age of the sediments as you dig deeper into it? What does this tell you about the age of tools that are embedded inside them?

4.   How old is this site? Why is this important?

5. What does this site tell us about the migration of
    ancient peoples to the New World?

The Bog People
of Windover, Florida

An early archeological site in Florida, known as the Windover archeological site, held important secrets as to who were the first peoples in the Americas. The long held theory that the first inhabitants to the North American continent arrived through a corridor between Siberia and Alaska, may be wrong.

The Windover bog offers a different story about the peopling of the Americas. The Windover bog, a muck pond located in the heart of Florida's central East coast swampland, contained about 168 human individuals that dated to 7,300 years ago. They were found buried in the peat at the bottom of the pond. Peat is decayed vegetation and organic matter that has accumulated over time. The pond, because of its anaerobic (lack of oxygen)

conditions and pH, preserved the skeletons and the brain tissue, of the individuals.

Scientists sequenced the DNA from the brain tissue and found some surprising results. This DNA, when compared to local native American tribes in the surrounding area do not match. These specimens had mitochondrial DNA, the haplotype X marker.

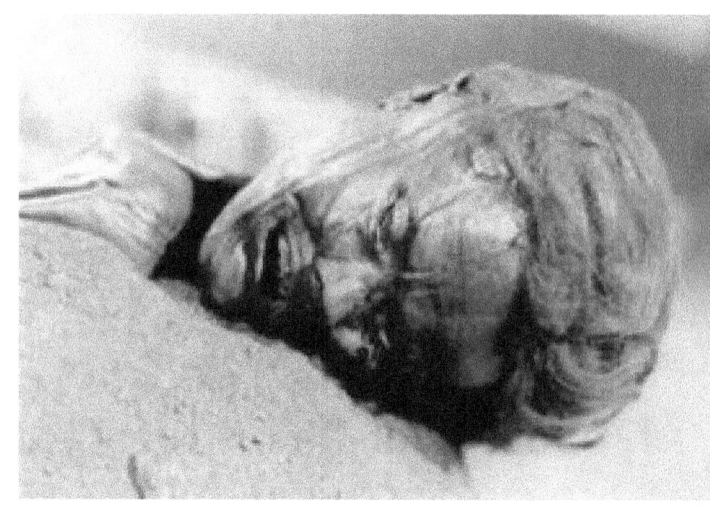

Haplotype X originally come from haplotype N which is found in the Levant, western Asia, and all throughout Europe. Most Native Americans from Siberia do not have haplotype X within their genome unless they mated with some who did and had offspring.

The beauty of analyzing genetic haplotypes or "genetic markers" from mitochondrial DNA is that specific migrating populations or groups of people can be tracked. Because mitochondrial DNA does not change much and is passed on from mother to child, it is a

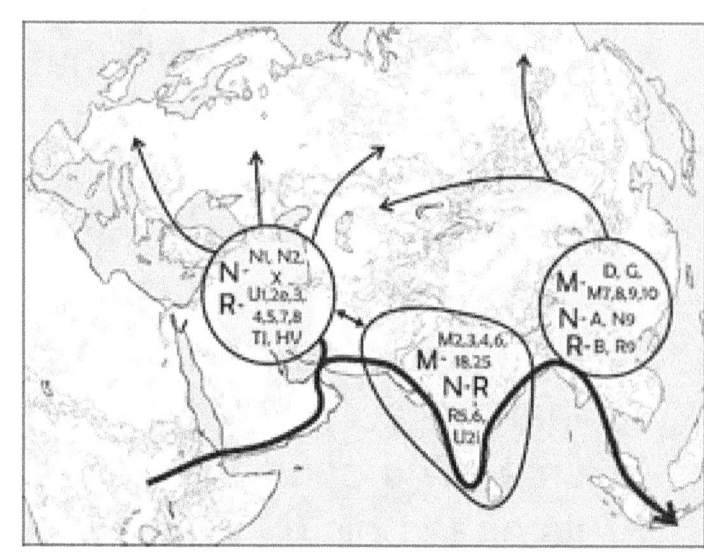

great source of genetic information to study. This information helps scientists to be able to place a population in a location on Earth within a specific period of time. The migration of these populations can then be followed by analyzing changes in the genetic markers. Only certain populations and groups of people will have "new" or recently developed genetic markers.

In this case, scientists have established that the members of the bog people of the Windover Bog site had European DNA. They have concluded that a migration, separate to that of the migration from Siberia, occurred. This population migrated from Europe into the North American continent.

Sources:

http://en.wikipedia.org/wiki/Windover_Archeological_Site
http://www.pbs.org/wgbh/nova/ancient/americas-bog-people.html
https://www.stormfront.org/forum/t937550/
http://en.wikipedia.org/wiki/Haplogroup_X_(mtDNA)

Focus Questions

1. What important event occurred at the Windover Bog Archeological site?

2. Describe the environmental conditions that preserved the individuals that were found at this site.

3. What evidence suggests that these individuals are not native Americans?

4. What specific genetic information proves that these individuals were of European decent?

5. Why are genetic markers useful to scientists?

6. Why are the findings of the Windover archeological site important?

The Clovis Culture

The **Clovis culture**, a paleo-indian culture who were located in Clovis New Mexico, was one of the first native American cultures to have settled in the Americas 13,200 years ago. Mainstream anthropologists and other scientists agree that they were the ancestors of many of the indigenous tribes in North America and Mexico. The Clovis culture first appeared after the last glacial period which marked the end of the ice age.

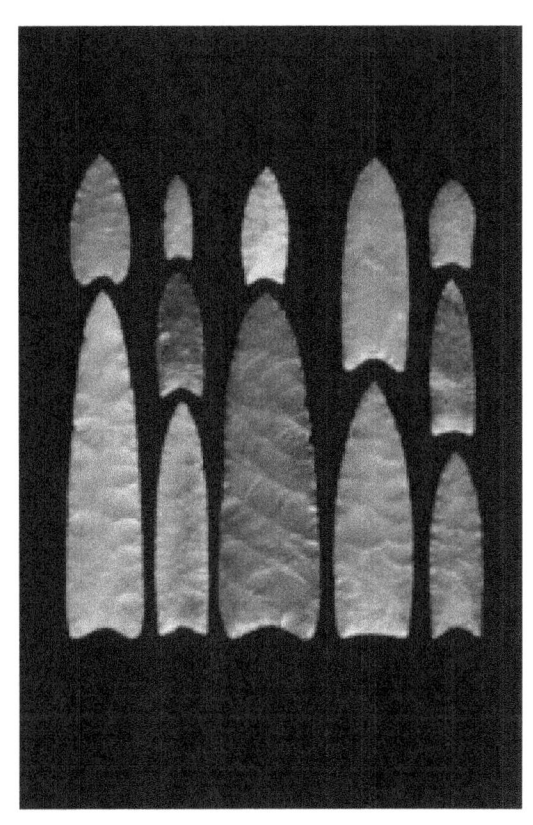

Several Clovis sites were discovered in the Americas. Some of these sites include Cactus Hill in Virginia, Paisley Caves in the Summer Lake Basin of Oregon, the Topper site in Allendale County, South Carolina, Meadowcroft Rockshelter in Pennsylvania, the Friedkin site in Texas, Cueva Fell in Chile and Monte Verde in Chile. It has been theorized that the Clovis sites on the east coast of the United States have European ancestry and

traveled into Canada from Northern Europe during the ice age. Over time, these people migrated down the east coast into Florida and along the southern United States, into Alabama, Mississippi, Louisiana, Texas, New Mexico, Arizona, and into Mexico. They also

migrated into Canada, the Great Lakes region, Wisconsin, Minnesota, Wyoming and Montana.

The tools of the Clovis culture are advanced and more sophisticated when compared to the tools of the Native Americans located in the Western United States and Canada. These tools include bifacial blades and spearpoints

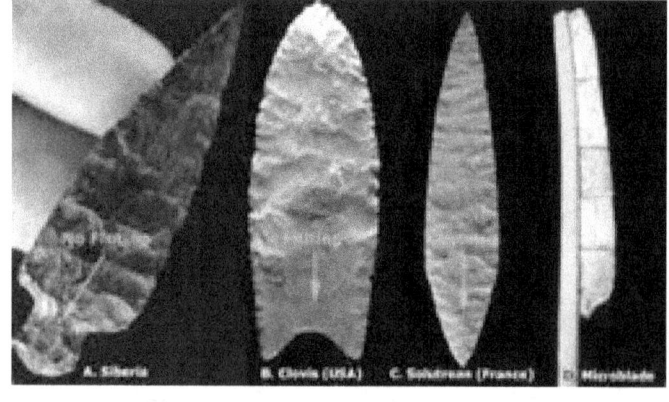

that are were made using pressure flaking. Pressure flaking is a technique of toolmaking that was heavily used in Spain and France up to 20,000 years ago.
The stone (chert) that was used for making spearpoints have been determined to have originated in France. This

evidence suggests that the first native people to have inhabited the Americas may have been of European decent.

Sources:

http://archaeology.about.com/od/clovispreclovis/qt/clovis_people.htm

Focus Questions:

1. Who were the Clovis culture?

2. Where are some of the Clovis sites in North America?

3. Describe the tools of the Clovis culture.

4. Where did the technique of pressure flaking originate? What can you infer about Clovis tools?

5. What conclusion can you draw between the tools of the Clovis culture in North America and the Solutrean culture of Europe?

Archeoastronomy

Archeoastronomy is the study of how the ancient people have understood the phenomena in the sky and how it was and incorporated used within their own cultures. Archeoastronomy was a common practice among the hunter-gatherers and civilizations all around the world. Archeoastronomy was incorporated **alignments** or the "lining up" of the sun, the moon, the planets, and the stars into earthen structures, buildings, the layouts of towns and cities,  and more importantly, into the traditions and rituals.

Archeoastronomy was first identified with ancient cultures who first started to practice agriculture and who first began to build permanent settlements in Africa, Europe, and Asia. Many archeological sites have also been discovered in the United States, such as the mound building sites that were constructed and occupied by the Native Americans 2000 to 3000 years ago. These archeological sites span from the Florida panhandle to the Mississippi River, and North to Wisconsin and is collectively known as the Mississipian culture.

One such **mound building** site that clearly used archeoastronomy is known as the Serpent Mound Site in Ohio. This an **effigy mound** site that was used for religious ceremonies and rituals. An effigy mound is a raised area of earth built in the shape of animals or symbols. Some of the mounds were used as burial mounds. The entrance to these burial mounds were aligned to the summer or winter solstices. Over 15,000 to 20,000 mounds were constructed.

The **Serpent Mound** is known to have at least 15 alignments to the sun and the moon. The site was built 2000 to 3000 years ago by an unknown group. It is the only serpent mound built in the United States. Although the identity of the mound builders is a mystery, it is clear that this culture had a high reverence for the serpent and may have engaged in ceremonies and rituals of serpent worship. In many ancient cultures, the serpent was a symbol of knowledge and it was also looked at as the "giver of life." The serpent was associated with the constellation Draco or "Dragon."

Knowledge and Comprehension
Words to Know:

Archeoastronomy:

Alignments:

Mound Building:

Effigy Mounds:

Serpent Mound:

1. What is archeoastronomy?

2. Where was archeoastronomy first used?

Application, Analysis, Evaluation and Synthesis

3. What is an effigy mound in your own words? Why did the ancient people in America build effigy mounds?

4. How was archeoastronomy incorporated into the Serpent Mound?

5. How was archeoastronomy incorporated as part of a culture's religious beliefs?

Ancient Wisdom:
Telling Time with Astronomy

Ancient cultures have been watching the heavens for thousands of years. They were world's first astronomers and scientists. They were able to track the movements of the sun, the moon, the stars, and the planets with relative accuracy throughout the millennia. They knew certain basic principles about astronomy, the study of the stars through their own observation, and were able to use this wisdom for many

purposes such as in the architecture, the lay out of their villages and towns, and long distance travel by land or by the sea.

Ancient cultures also figured out how to tell time and identify the seasons using their knowledge of the sky. To help them with this, they constructed **stone circles** (also known as henges). A **stone circle** is a collection of stones, arranged in a circular pattern on the ground, that marks the positions and the movements of the sun, moon, stars, and planets over time. Stone circles enabled ancient people to track the passage of time and predict the movements of heavenly bodies and astronomical events such as the eclipses of the sun and the moon into the future.

A stone circle could also be used to find the **cardinal directions** (North, South, East and West) using the movement of the sun and the position of the pole star. If you know where due North is, you were able to establish the other directions such as South, East and West. Ancient people were able to find due North in the night time sky by identifying the pole star. The **pole star,** in the Northern Hemisphere today, is Polaris. It is this star that marks the location of the North Pole. This star seems to be fixed at this location, and all the other stars in the night time sky move in a circular motion around the pole star.

The other cardinal directions are easy to find if the location of the pole star is known. South was exactly opposite of North. If you faced in the direction of the pole star, it would be directly behind you. Both North and South lie of the same axis on the Earth, in a straight line. Ancient people created the north-south axis on the ground by putting a stone on ground to mark the position of the pole star and placing two more stones, one above and one below the stone marker used to mark the position of the pole star. Both were equidistant or equal in distance from this marker.

The directions of West and East could be established by watching the sunrise and the sunset. The sun rises in the east and sets in the west. If you were to position yourself at the position marking the pole star and faced North, east and west could be marked on the ground by putting a marker where the sun rises and a marker where the sun sets. Both of these stones are placed equidistant from the marker representing the North pole.

Focus Questions:

1. What kind of knowledge did the ancient cultures use to tell time?

2. Explain why the ancient cultures were known as the "first scientists"

3. What is a stone circle?

4. Explain how they were constructed or built.

5. Explain how to determine the cardinal directions using a stone circle.

6. Build a stone circle out of stones in your back yard to keep track of the sun. Place a pencil or a stick in the center of the stone circle. With chalk, draw the shadow it makes on the ground at 8am, 12 pm, and 4pm. Label each shadow with the time. Write down your observations. Is there a pattern?

Native American Glyphs

Native Americans used glyphs or pictures to communicate an idea or a concept. Glyphs were used by many cultures around the world, before the invention of writing, as a way to communicate and record their thoughts. Early cultures first used the surfaces stones and rock walls as a blank canvas to engrave their glyphs on.

In this activity, you will learn about some of the glyphs that were used by the native Americans and be able to use these glyphs to communicate on your own.

Instructions:

1. Study the glyphs and their meanings on the 3 pages that are included in this activity.

2. On a white piece of paper, translate the following sentences into glyphs.

a. We eat fish, ducks and deer.

b. I discovered a meteor in the evening sky. I was afraid.

c. I will use a stone hammer to build a house by the River.

d. Sing and use drum and stick around the fire campfire.

e. There are bird tracks and deer tracks in the direction of mountain.

3. Make a message of your own using the glyphs. Share this message with others and have them translate them.

4. **Make Your Own Petroglyph:** on a ceramic tile, etch air carve your message on the surface of the tile with a sharp rock or stone.

Deer, Moose	Direction	Discovery	Dog	Duck
Eagle	Eagle Tail	Eat	Encampment	Evening
Famine	Fear	Fear	Fire	Camp Fire
Fish	Peace Flag	Grave Flag	Plenty Food	Fort
Fox	Black Fox	Froze to Death	Girl	Goods
Goose	Grasp	Gun	White Hawk	Heart
Hard	Hear	Hit	Horse	Spotted Horse
Horse Tracks	Hungry	Stole Horses	Fast Horse	Ropes Horses

ANTELOPE   ARROWS   BEAR ALIVE   BEAR DEAD   BEAVER   BIRD TRACKS

CAMP   CANOE   CROW   FIRE (CAMP)   FISH   FORT

HORSE TRACKS   GUN   BLANKET   EAGLE   HORSE   EAT

SEE   DEEP SNOW   MOUNTAIN   KNIFE   LIGHTNING   PIPE   HEART

BUFFALO   RAN   NIGHT   DAY   RAIN   LIFE   SPEAK   SNAKE

RIVER   WAR   CORN   FIFTEEN   SMALLPOX   TREE   HUNGRY   CANOE WITH WARRIORS

MAKING PEACE   3 DAYS   DEER TRACKS   DUCK   HEAR   HUNT   CACHE, MANY   A LOT OF MEAT

STARS   SKY   WINTER   OLD   MEDICINE MAN   WAR BONNET   TOMAHAWK

Cactus	Canyon	Christian	Corn	Dead
Drum and Stick	Drumstick	Earth Lodge	Geese	Grass
Stone Hammer	I did it.	Hidden, Obscure	House.	I or Me.
Inspired.	Meteor.	Moon (new hump)	Moon (reached half)	Moon (full).
Mouse.	Old.	Otter.	Prayer	Prisoner.
Shining, Bright	Singing	Snow.	Strong.	Rising Sun.
Supplication.	Talk (intense)	Thunder Bird.	Travois.	Old Tree.
Turkey.	Turtle.	Walk.	War.	Woods.

Pictogrphs by William Tomkins

What is a Petroglyph?

A **petroglyph** or rock engraving is an ancient picture that has been created on the surface of a rock or stone. The word petroglyph is a greek word meaning "carved rock" The surface of the rock or stone is carved and picked using a sharp tool. Many early cultures around the world used hard stones with sharp edges or bones to create images and symbols, depicting their ideas, real life events, and their religious beliefs. The oldest petroglyphs found on Earth are 27,000 years old and were found in Australia.

Many of the petroglyphs that are found represent the life of prehistoric peoples. Scenes of successful hunts showing human figures and or the animals they hunted such as big horn sheep, antelope or wild animals seen while they were huntingsuch as horses and coyotes, decorate many rock walls that can still be seen today.

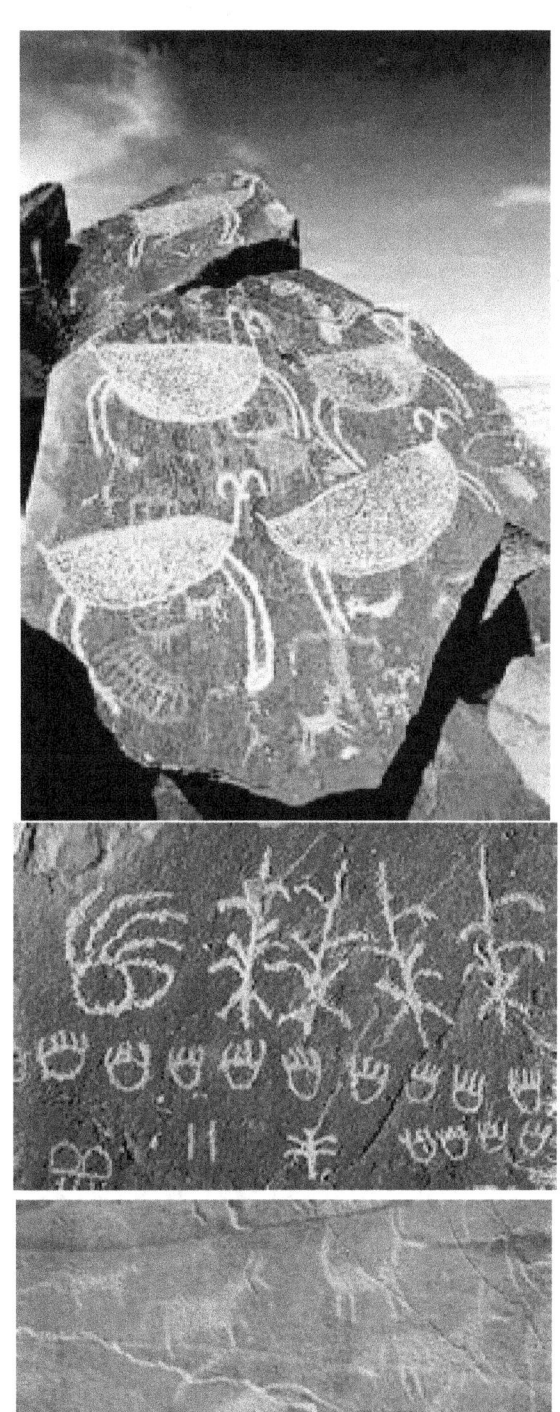

Some of these types of petroglyphs also depict family life as well. Some petroglyphs are a representation of the members of a family such as the father, the mother, and a child.

Another use for petroglyphs is for honoring and paying respect to their Gods. The Gods of some native American Gods do not look human, but look other worldly. This representation is based on the belief that their Gods came to them from the heavens, from distant stars. They would have ceremonies lead by their spiritual leaders or shamans, and they would pray to these Gods for guidance and their protection.

Some petroglyphs were maps that used symbols as a form of early communication, as a form of communication before writing was invented or used. Different symbols were used to represent distances, time, the local terrain, landforms such as mountains, rivers, and animal life such as trees and different animals native to the area.

Sources:

http://judacullarock.com/

http://en.wikipedia.org/wiki/Judaculla_Rock
http://www-personal.umich.edu/~artsfx/
paintingx0802judaculla3.html

Focus Questions:

1. Explain what a petroglyph is.

2. What are most petroglyphs made of?

3. How were petroglyphs made?

4. Why did ancient cultures create petroglyphs?

5. Why were petroglyphs important to ancient cultures?

6. Imagine you were an ancient hunter who just came back from a successful hunt. Draw a petroglyph about where you went to hunt and what animals you hunted.

Animism

Animism many ancient cultures, as well as the Native

Americans, believe in animism. Animism is a worldview that all living and non-living things have a **soul** or a **spirit**. It is was used as the basis of some of religious and belief systems of the indigenous people and groups of the past and also in the present. It was widespread in primitive and ancient societies before the onset of organized religion.

Animism describes the most common threads of the spiritual and supernatural viewpoints and perspectives of ancient cultures and group. There is no separation between the physical and the spiritual worlds. There is no separation between people, animals, plants and their environment. They are all connected to each other and influence each other seamlessly.

All the souls and the spirits of living and nonliving things exist together on the Earth. They believe that these souls and spirits could be called upon for guidance, protection, and for the betterment of daily life. Animism can be found in Shinto, Serer, Hinduism, Buddhism, Scientology, Jainism, Paganism, and Neopaganism.

One example of this is a widely held Native American belief that people do not "own" the land. In many of their languages, their is no word for "ownership." This is because the land has a soul or a spirit. It is its own entity which should be respected and taken care of. The Native Americans connect with the energy of this spirit and live in harmony with it in order to benefit from the land. Land is sacred to them because it helps to nurture and protect them.

It was theorized by anthropologists that societies that became more scientifically advanced over time, abandoned animism for more organized religions. This may be because as societies became more self-reliant, their reliance and need for communicating and interacting with the souls and spirits for supernatural intervention began to decrease overtime. This could be the result of an increase of knowledge and understanding for scientific and natural phenomena through scientific advancement. As more questions were answered and more explanations were made through scientific knowledge and understanding, a shift in the beliefs of the supernatural and spiritual world may have occurred. Their material needs and their lifestyles changed as well. Some of these societies moved

in a different direction according to their new beliefs which may explain why more scientifically advanced societies began to follow organized religions.

Sources:

http://en.wikipedia.org/wiki/Animism

Focus Questions:

1. What is animism?

2. Who believed in animism? Who still believes in animism?

3. What is an example of animism?

4. How is animism beneficial?

5. Explain why some societies moved away from animism.

Shamanism

In ancient times, the early people around the world, believed that nature and the universe were controlled by the spirit world. They saw that the sky was filled with celestial bodies such as the sun, the moon, the planets, and stars that moved from one place to another each day and night. They closely watched and paid attention to these heavenly movements and believed that their motion was caused by "spirits" that controlled them. They also believed that all things on Earth, living and nonliving, had spirits associated with them as well. This was the earliest form of religion and spiritual beliefs shared by early humans and dates back at least 30,000 - 40,000 years ago in Europe and the New World.

Many cultures in the past and the present, especially native American tribes, had shamans or people who were known as "spiritual healers" or "medicine men." They, like priests,

rabbis, and other religious leaders, would be in communication with the "great spirit," (God), and other spirits. They made direct contact with the spirit world while in an altered state of consciousness, and channeled energy from these spirits back into the world. This contact would occur on behalf of physically and mentally sick people as a way to heal them. They believed if the soul is healed, physical ailments would also be healed. Physical illness was caused by traumas affecting the soul. Shamans helped to balance the soul and its energy, and to restore physical health. They also contacted the spirits to ask them questions, ask for help, and to predict events that could occur in the future on behalf of others and the community.

Sources:

http://en.wikipedia.org/wiki/Shamanism

Focus Questions:

1. What did the early cultures believe about nature and the universe?

2. What did the early cultures believe about the movement of the sun, moon, planets, and the stars?

3. What is a shaman?

4. Describe how a shaman heals people.

5. Explain why shamans contact the "spirits"?

6.   Do you think that a way they could have explained the movements of celestial bodies was by believing that they were controlled by "spirits"? Why or why not?